Social Skills
Activities for Kids

SOCIAL SKILLS

ACTIVITIES

for Kids

50 Fun Activities for Making Friends, Talking and Listening, and Understanding Social Rules

Natasha Daniels, LCSW

Illustrated by Sarah Rebar

ROCKRIDGE PRESS

Interior and Cover Designer: Suzanne LaGasa
Photo Art Director: Sue Bischofberger
Editor: Susan Randol
Production Editor: Andrew Yackira

Author Photo © Paul Hill
Illustration © 2019 Sarah Rebar

ISBN: Print 978-1-64152-296-0 | eBook 978-1-64152-297-7

To Chloe, Xander, and Alexis,

who make my life sparkle.

Contents

Introduction
FOR PARENTS

As a parent, you know that **EVERY CHILD IS UNIQUE**. They all come with their own amazing talents, skills, and personalities. Some kids are awesome at math, while other kids might need a little tutoring. Some kids can pick up a pencil and draw from their imagination, while other kids could use some coaching.

Just as with language, math, or art, kids have different abilities when it comes to social skills. Some children can intuitively sense how other people are feeling, while other children might need to develop those skills. Some kids naturally make friends, while others need to be taught skills on how to develop friendships. You are probably very much aware of where your child stands in this area, and where they could use some help. I'm here to tell you that this stuff can be learned—and it can really change a kid's confidence level and success in social situations.

And as with teaching math concepts or reading comprehension, social skills can be broken down into bite-size pieces that your child can digest and learn from. With this book and you as a supportive guide, your child can develop the essential social skills needed to be socially successful at school, in family situations, and out and about in the community.

Like any other skill, practice makes perfect. So I encourage you to read along, then help your child learn the skills outlined in this book and do the activities with them. Your child may be able to do them alone, but the skills taught in this book will become more solidified if you partner with your child to help them along the way.

Your child didn't learn how to read overnight—you remember how it took time and practice. They had to learn their letters before they could learn their words. Social skills are very much the same way. Your child will learn the building blocks of social interactions one step at a time, and each block will build on another.

It's also important to remember that kids learn at their own pace. Some kids will take these skills and run with them, while others might take some more time. Don't forget to celebrate the small steps along the way with high-fives, fist bumps, words of encouragement, and hugs! These small steps lead to big changes over time.

If your child continues to struggle even after working through the activities in this book, don't be afraid to consider professional help. A good child therapist can offer ongoing support and guidance to help you and your child navigate through these issues.

Now let's stop all this chitchat and get busy arming your child with social skills for confidence and success, shall we?

Hello, FRIEND!

MAKING FRIENDS CAN BE HARD. I know—really hard. It can be frustrating watching everyone around you make friends while you continue to struggle. I get it! When I was a child, my family moved around often. I found myself constantly in new schools, surrounded by new faces. I didn't know how to make friends. I waited hopelessly, wishing someone would approach me and try to be my friend. It rarely happened, so I often felt awkward and alone.

I don't want that to be your story. I wish someone had helped me build my confidence. I wish someone had encouraged me to make some brave moves. I wish someone had taught me how to start and keep conversations going, even with people I didn't know.

People with great social skills aren't in a secret club that you can't be a part of, even though it can feel that way sometimes. You can learn social skills! I didn't have this book, but eventually I learned how to grow my social skills. I learned what things were holding me back and how to fight through my fears. I even learned how to start conversations and finally, thankfully, how to make and keep friendships going.

Luckily, you don't have to wait as long as I did to get your social skill wings! I have written this book to teach you all the social skills you'll need right now to thrive in school, at home, and around the neighborhood.

First, I will teach you how to figure out what skills you already have, and what skills you will want to develop. I'm going to help you learn how to make friends and keep friends, and how to handle all the strange things that can happen in between (like when to tell on others, how to handle gossip, and tons more). And the best part? We are going to do it in a fun, sometimes silly way, because learning new skills should never be boring!

One thing: It is important that you go through this book in order. Have you ever built a tower of blocks? Each block holds the other one up, right? Well, the same is true about this book. I've included 50 activities, which are things you can do on your own or with a family member. You will also find bonus activities that will help you test out your social skills in social situations. Each skill you learn builds on top of another. So if you want your tower to be strong and solid, don't skip any of the building blocks in this book. Do one activity at a time and then move on to the next one.

Okay, one other thing: You can't be a great ninja if you practice your ninja moves only once a month, right? Well, you also can't rock your social skills if you don't practice them. Practice makes perfect. So don't forget to do all your activities and practice the skills I teach you in each one.

Do you want to know who is awesome? You! Because you want to supercharge your social skills, and you are taking a giant step in the right direction.

Are you ready to get started? Let's do this!

Chapter One

WHAT ARE SOCIAL SKILLS

(AND WHO CARES ABOUT THEM, ANYWAY)?

Do you ever wonder why it is so easy for some kids to make friends? Does it seem like everyone has a secret handbook on how to behave and act—except you? Trust me, there is no secret handbook and no secret sauce. The real trick is to know and understand *social skills*. Social skills are like superpowers, except that anyone can use them if they know how. Social skills help you know how to talk to people and how to behave at home, in school, and around your neighborhood. To answer the question, "Who cares about them, anyway?" you will soon learn that the answer is *pretty much everybody*! As with any skill, sometimes people need to learn and practice social skills to become a social skills master. And that's exactly what we are going to do in this book. So let's get started!

DECODE YOUR SOCIAL SKILL SUPERPOWERS

Why are social skills like superpowers? Because they can tell us so much about what is going on in any particular situation. Our social skill superpowers are always at work. We just need to pay attention to them! There are three main ways our superpowers get information—through what we *see, hear,* and *feel.*

Our superpowers help us understand what is happening, so we can decide how to act.

Let's learn how your superpowers work. Once you see how they work, you'll want to try them in new social situations as well.

Directions

Look at the picture and answer the questions that follow.

What do you see?

- -

- -

- -

- -

- -

- -

What do you hear?

What do you feel?

Based on what you see, hear, and feel, what do you guess is going on in this picture?

What do you think the girl sitting down needs right now?

If you were on the field with her, what would you do?

BONUS ACTIVITY

. . . .

Start thinking about your social skill superpowers. When watching kids at school or in the neighborhood, pay attention to exactly what you think is going on through what you see, hear, and feel.

GOING BLINDFOLDED

Have you ever tried to walk around blindfolded? If you did, you probably bumped into a lot of things. You might have even guessed you were in a completely different room! Not having social skills is kind of like being blindfolded. We need social skills to help guide us when we're with other people and talking to them. Social skills also help us know what to say, when to say it, and even how to say it. Can you imagine not having the skills to do any of that? Without social skills, we'd be lost!

Do you want to see what I mean?

What you need

* Someone in your family
* Something to cover your eyes

Directions

Cover your eyes and walk around your room. Try to find the doorknob. Make sure that someone is in the room watching you to make sure you don't get hurt.

Was it easy to get around your room?
Did you bump into things?
Did you feel lost?

That's kind of how it would feel to not have any social skills. Luckily, you already have some social skills, and throughout this book you are going to develop, grow, and sharpen your social skills even more. There will be no blindfolds for you when it comes to social skills—in fact, you will learn to use all your senses to know what to do!

WHEN TO USE YOUR SUPERPOWERS

The cool thing about social skills is that we are using them even when we don't know we are using them. That's weird, right? We are constantly watching, hearing, and feeling what is going on around us. What you see, hear, and feel can give you clues about what to do next.

Let's see how these clues help you out.

Directions

Read the following social situations. In the column next to each one, write which social skill superpower will help you the most: seeing, hearing, or feeling. (Hint: It can be all three!)

SOCIAL SITUATION	SOCIAL SKILL SUPERPOWER USED [WRITE SEE, HEAR, AND/OR FEEL]
You are sitting in class and someone is crying behind you.	
You are playing with three friends. One friend has his head down and a frown on his face.	
You are at lunch and a bunch of kids are talking about your favorite video game.	
A student is asking everyone around her if she can borrow a pencil.	
A bunch of girls are teasing a boy. His face gets red and his eyes tear up.	

WHEN TO USE YOUR SUPERPOWERS, *continued*

SOCIAL SITUATION	SOCIAL SKILL SUPERPOWER USED [WRITE SEE, HEAR, AND/OR FEEL]
You call out the answer in class without raising your hand, and your teacher scolds you in front of everyone.	
Your teacher's hands are full, and she is trying to open the door.	
Everyone is playing tag except the new girl sitting alone on the grass.	

Look at your responses. Which social skill superpower do you use the most? Do you pay attention to what you see the most? Hear? Or feel? Maybe you do all three, or a combination of two of them?

Write down which ones you use the most in social situations, and which ones you want to develop and grow.

- -

- -

- -

- -

- -

- -

WHAT'S THE STORY?

The more you use your social skill superpowers, the better they will become. I want to teach you how to be more observant, aware, and tuned in to what's happening around you. When you spend time watching, listening, and sharing the feelings of those around you, your superpowers will explode!

You can practice sharpening your skills all the time, even when you're just sitting somewhere. One of my favorite things to do is "people watch." People can be so interesting. Why are they making that face? What is making them run so fast? Are they late? What is that couple arguing about? Why is that little girl crying? Trying to figure out why people are doing what they're doing is a good way to practice your social skill superpowers.

Directions

Let's practice tuning in to what is going on. Below are situations that cause different emotions. Copy them onto small pieces of paper, fold each one, and put them in a bowl. Ask a few family members to play Emotion Charades with you. Pick out a situation from the bowl, but don't tell anyone what you got. Act it out without using any words. Can they guess what is going on? Did they guess the right emotion? Take turns being the one acting and the one guessing.

You are scared because you are lost.	You are angry you can't go to the party.
You are excited you got a present.	You are upset you lost your favorite book.
You are sad because your friend moved to a different school.	You are stressed out about a project.
You are happy you got a great grade on a test.	You are hurt that you weren't included in a playground game.
You are surprised by your grandparents' visit.	You are annoyed that you have to clean your room.

WHAT'S THE STORY?, *continued*

There are mysteries and stories all around us, all the time.

    If you want to grow your powers to notice what is happening around you, play this simple game.

BONUS ACTIVITY

· ·

Go to a public place. This can be the park, a restaurant, your school—practically anywhere will work. Sit quietly in one spot and open up your eyes, ears, and heart.

    Find a person or people to watch and observe.

    In your imagination or on the lines provided, make up a story about what you think is going on.

What did you *see* that helped you make up your story?

What did you *hear* that helped you make up your story?

What did you *feel* that helped you make up your story?

When you become observant and really notice what is happening around you, you will become a better friend. If you see a friend who is in a hurry, you won't keep them waiting. If you notice a friend who isn't playing at recess, you will take the time to make sure they're okay. The more observant you are, the more tuned in you'll be to those around you.

TOP 10 EVERYDAY SOCIAL SKILLS

It may seem like there are an awful lot of social skills to learn. Some you'll use every now and then, and some you'll use all the time. Here's a quick list of the top 10 social skills that you can use every day:

1. Be friendly and smile at others.

2. Be considerate and thoughtful of those around you. This includes not touching others without asking.

3. Share and wait your turn.

4. Be calm and control your emotions, especially anger.

5. Don't talk unkindly about other people.

6. Ask people questions about themselves.

7. Ask other people to play with you.

8. Have good manners and be polite.

9. Make good eye contact and don't mumble.

10. Don't hog the conversation. Take turns talking and listening.

MY SUPERPOWER SCORE

By now you should have a good idea about what all the fuss is around social skills. Just as in math, writing, or art, we all have our talents. Some of us are great at math, and some of us (like me!) have to really practice. Some of us are awesome at drawing, and some of us have to be taught how to draw well.

Social skills are the same way. Some people have great social skills, and some of us have to learn how to improve our superpowers. Either way it's okay, because learning these skills is fun and really easy to do.

Let's figure out how you feel about your own social skills right now, so we can discover where you want to grow. This will also help you see all the superpowers you stand to gain by the end of our time together in this book.

Directions

Read each social skill superpower and put a check mark where you think you are. Don't worry if you have some areas you need help on—that's what this book is for! If you can think of other social skills not mentioned here, fill them in at the bottom.

SOCIAL SKILL	NEED HELP	PRETTY GOOD	DOING GREAT!
Talking to kids I know			
Talking to kids I don't know			
Talking to adults I know			
Talking to adults I don't know			

MY SUPERPOWER SCORE, *continued*

SOCIAL SKILL	NEED HELP	PRETTY GOOD	DOING GREAT!
Starting a conversation			
Entering a group conversation			
Keeping a conversation going			
Ending a conversation			
Making new friends			
Playing/hanging out with others			
Keeping friendships going			
Making plans with friends			
Raising my hand at school			
Asking for help			

SOCIAL SKILL	NEED HELP	PRETTY GOOD	DOING GREAT!
Standing up for others			
Talking to a friend's parent			
Feeling comfortable at a friend's house			
Feeling comfortable at sleepovers			
Fill in:			
Fill in:			

Look at your results. You may have areas you're doing great in, and others you're not comfortable with yet. That's fine! In this book, you will find activities that focus on skills you already have, and some that will target skills that you may need help improving. But even if you don't need help in a certain area, it's still a good idea to do all the activities. A little extra practice is always useful, and you may learn something new anyway—even if you're already good at it! However, be sure to pay extra-close attention to the activities where you need some help. In fact, it can even help to go back later and revisit those activities from time to time to continue to grow and strengthen those skills.

WHAT HOLDS ME BACK?

Have you ever told yourself, *I can't do this*?! Many of us lose some of our superpowers because of the things we tell ourselves. What we tell ourselves can have incredible power over us. It can make us scared in situations that aren't really scary and, worse yet, it can make us give up before we even begin.

What kinds of situations make you feel doubtful? What situations do you avoid? What do you think might be holding you back from joining conversations, being in social situations, or even making friends? Do you have fears that are bubbling under the surface?

Directions

Fill in the following thought bubbles with some of your biggest worries around social situations or making friends. Write your worries in red. Now go back and write a positive thought in green. Sometimes when we change the way we look at things, we can make ourselves feel much more confident.

Example:

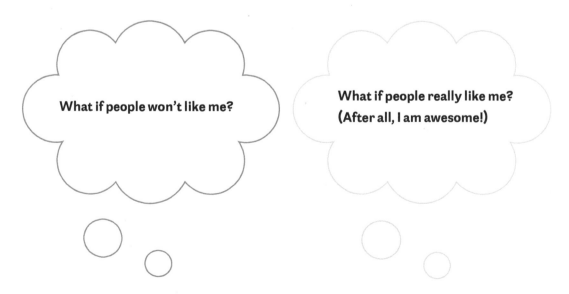

What if people won't like me?

What if people really like me?
(After all, I am awesome!)

YOU CRACKED THE CODE!

Hey, awesome sauce! You just finished your first chapter and, believe it or not, you are well on your way to creating some amazing social skill superpowers!

Think about what you've already learned. You now know that:

- Social skills are like superpowers that help us wherever we go
- Social sKills involve what we see, hear, and feel
- Social skills can be learned and practiced

You also know some new things about yourself:

- What social skills you have that are already strong, and which ones you want to grow
- What fears you may have around being social and making and keeping friends, and how you can shift your thinking from negative to positive

But this party is just getting started! In chapter 2, you're going to learn how to talk to everybody and anybody. That means exploring how to:

- Start a conversation
- Keep a conversation going
- Know what questions to ask
- Keep from being bossy
- End a conversation

Conversation skills can be tricky for many kids, but I'll walk you through them, one step at a time.

Chapter Two

HOW TO TALK TO ANYBODY . . . AND EVERYBODY!

Learning how to talk to people is a bit like riding a bike for the first time. It can seem tricky. With a bike, you might need some training wheels, so you can practice riding while building your confidence. As you go, you might worry you'll fall off and get hurt. You might get frustrated that it seems as if everyone around you can ride with ease. You might even want to give up or just completely avoid it! But just be patient—once you master how to do it, riding a bike becomes super easy.

Guess what? The same goes with learning how to talk to people. It can be scary at first. You might be thinking, *How do I start a conversation? What should I ask? How does a conversation end? What if my feelings get hurt?*

But when you learn how to talk to people one step at a time, one small pedal at a time, it won't seem as scary. Before you know it, you'll say, *What was all that worrying about? I can totally do this!* When you do things in small bites, building skills of any kind can lead to big changes and awesome progress. So let's go take some small bites and get you on your way!

CONVERSATION STARTERS

Starting a conversation can be overwhelming. What should you say? Think of it this way: Just as you might plan your moves in soccer before the actual game, planning your conversation starters before an actual conversation can make you feel more prepared. A conversation starter is a question you can ask someone to get a conversation going. Asking a question about someone's interests is a great way to get a conversation going. People LOVE talking about themselves!

Give it a try—can you come up with some good conversation starters for these situations?

A classmate is holding a ball and standing alone on the playground.

- -

- -

A neighbor is walking his dog.

- -

- -

A friend comes over to your house to play.

- -

- -

If you came up with ideas, great! If you are still not sure what to ask, that's okay, too—I've got you covered. Read on!

BONUS ACTIVITY

Here are a few possible conversation starters. Pick one of my suggestions from the list and do a social experiment. Go up to someone you know and try out one of the conversation starters on them. It's better to try out new skills on people you know at first.

Once you've completed your social experiment, come back and answer the questions that follow.

Pick one of these conversation starters to try:

- How was your weekend? What did you do?
- Do you play [insert your favorite video game or hobby]? What's your favorite video game [or hobby]?
- Do you watch [insert your favorite TV show]? What's your favorite thing to watch?
- Do you have any pets? What are their names?
- I like your shirt [or other object]. Where did you get it?

Did you do it? How did it go?

Who did you ask?

- -

What was the person's response?

- -

How did you feel asking the question?

- -

The more practice you get starting conversations, the easier it will become!

GOLDILOCKS AND THE THREE QUESTIONS

Asking people questions can be a good thing! It shows that you're interested in them and that you care about what they have to say. But finding the right amount of questions to ask is important. When you ask too many questions, you might seem nosy. When you ask too few questions, it might seem like you don't care.

Do you remember the story about Goldilocks and the three bears? One porridge was too hot, one was too cold, and one was just right.

Let's play a new version of that. Below are three conversations. One shows a boy asking too many questions, one shows a boy asking too few questions, and one shows a boy asking just the right number.

Directions

Next to each conversation, circle if you think the questions Tom asks are **Too Few**, **Too Many**, or **Just Right**.

1. Tom saw that his friend John was wearing a cast on his leg. Tom went up to the boy and asked, "What happened?" John said he fell. Tom asked, "On what?" John responded, "Off my bed." Tom asked, "How on earth did that happen?" John said, "I rolled off." Tom replied, "How can you just roll off your bed?"

   Too Few / **Too Many** / **Just Right**

2. Tom saw that his friend John was wearing a cast on his leg. Tom went up to John and asked, "Do you want to play?" John said, "Okay."

   Too Few / **Too Many** / **Just Right**

3. Tom saw that his friend John was wearing a cast on his leg. Tom went up to John and asked, "What happened?" John said he fell. Tom asked, "On what?" John responded, "Off my bed." Tom said, "I'm sorry that happened. I hope it gets better soon."

   Too Few / **Too Many** / **Just Right**

Answer Key

1. Too many. 2. Too few. 3. Just right.

BONUS ACTIVITY

Start paying attention to how many questions you ask people around you. If you think you are starting to ask too many, pull back and become a good listener. If you think you don't typically ask enough questions, start pushing yourself to ask a few more. With practice this will start to feel natural for you.

Just as you want to ask the right number of questions, it's also important to ask questions that are appropriate. When Tom asked John, "How can you just roll off your bed?" that question was not just "too much," it was also a little unkind and really did not consider John's feelings.

When you practice asking questions, try to put yourself in the listener's shoes. Think about this: *Is the question I'm asking* **kind**? *Is the question I'm asking* **necessary**? When you put yourself in someone else's shoes, you're able to understand how they feel when they hear your questions. And this makes you a better friend!

THROW IT BACK!

Do you want to learn a cool ninja trick to keep conversations going? This is going to sound kind of silly, but it really works! Anytime someone asks you a question, just throw it back. Think about playing catch: What do you do when someone throws you the ball? You throw it back.

The same can happen in conversations. It's easy. If someone asks you a question, you answer and then throw back the same question to them. Remember, people like talking about themselves. Asking questions is a great way to make people know you care, and a simple way to do that is by throwing back questions that are thrown at you.

For example, if someone asks you:

What are you doing over summer break?

You would throw it back with something like:

I'm going to camp. What are you doing over summer break?

Simple enough, right? Okay, your turn. Let's give it a spin.

Directions

For each question below, throw back a question. Write your answers in the space provided.

How are you?

How was your weekend?

THROW IT BACK!, *continued*

What did you do last night?

- -

- -

Did you do the homework?

- -

- -

What are you doing at recess?

- -

- -

Pretty simple, right?

KEEP THE CONVERSATION BALL MOVING

Remember how we talked about throwing questions back in our last activity? Well, in this activity we are going to continue playing ball, but we're going to add some new skills. Once again, think about conversations as a game of catch. When you play catch, you don't just sit there and hold the ball, right? No, that would be rude. Instead, you throw the ball back.

The same thing happens with conversations. When someone throws you the ball by asking you a question, it's your job to answer and then throw the ball back by asking them a question. That's how you keep a conversation going.

Let's break it down:

1. Someone throws you the ball (they ask you a question)
    Them: How was your weekend?

2. You hold the ball (and answer their question)
    You: It was good, thanks. We went to the football game.

3. You throw the ball back (and ask them a question)
    You: Did you go to the game? OR What did **YOU** do this weekend?

Do you see how you can take the time to answer the question and then throw back a question? The question can be the exact question they asked you (as we did in activity 9) or a new question related to how you answered their question.

Let's practice!

KEEP THE CONVERSATION BALL MOVING, *continued*

Directions

Play conversation ball and fill in the blanks with how you could answer. Remember to answer the other person's question and then offer up a question to them.

1. Them: How did you do on that math test?
    Your response:

    -

    The question you throw back:

    -

2. Them: Did you hear the storm last night?
    Your response:

    -

    The question you throw back:

    -

3. Them: What are you doing this summer?
    Your response:

    -

    The question you throw back:

    -

BONUS ACTIVITY

· ·

For bonus points, try this skill in the real world. The next time someone asks you a question, try to see how long you can bounce the conversation ball back. Keeping a conversation going is an awesome skill to add to your social skill superpowers—it helps you get to know others, make friends, and let people know you are fun to talk to.

INTERRUPTION EXPERIMENT

Interrupting someone while they are talking can really ruin a conversation. It's too bad, because people don't usually interrupt on purpose. People interrupt for all sorts of reasons. Here are just a few:

- They have something important to say
- They don't want to forget what they were going to say
- They are upset and want to get their point in
- They aren't paying attention to what the other person is saying

Regardless of the reason, it can make the other person feel upset. Have you ever been interrupted when you were speaking? How did it make you feel?

Let's test out what happens when you interrupt.

Directions

Sometimes you may not realize how it seems when you are constantly interrupting someone. It can be hard for us to put ourselves in someone else's shoes—especially when we are talking.

Read the conversation here, and then answer the questions that follow.

BRAD: *I love that video game! I play that all the time.*

SARAH: *Me, too.*

BRAD: *Did you get the latest update?*

SARAH: *Yeah, I just…*

BRAD: *I did. It is so much better than the last one.*

SARAH: *I know, I was playing it and…*

BRAD: *I got past level 5 last night and I've only been playing it for two days.*

SARAH: *Oh wow—what's…*

BRAD: *The controls are so much easier in this version.*

SARAH: *I know. I thought the…*

BRAD: *I wonder when the next version will come out. Maybe next year?*

INTERRUPTION EXPERIMENT, *continued*

How do you think Sarah felt throughout this conversation?

Do you think Sarah enjoyed talking to Brad? Why or why not?

What could Brad have done differently?

BONUS ACTIVITY

Start a conversation with someone in your family. Tell them you are going to do an experiment, then ask them some questions to get the conversation going. Interrupt them three times as they start to talk. Come back and answer the following questions. (Don't forget to tell them at the end you were doing an experiment on interrupting, and to please excuse you for frustrating them!)

What expression did they have on their face?

Did they seem to get more and more frustrated?

Did they grow annoyed or angry at you?

Did they eventually stop trying to talk to you?

It's helpful to be aware of how often you interrupt others. Many kids (and grown-ups, too!) aren't aware that they are even doing this. Once you start paying attention to how often you interrupt, you can build up your skills around being patient, listening, and taking turns—all great ways to make and keep friends.

NO ONE'S THE BOSS OF US!

Do you know what it means to be bossy? When someone is being bossy, they tell you what to do and maybe even *how* to do it. They don't give you a chance to do what you want to do or be who you want to be. Sounds pretty bad, don't you think? But sometimes we can be bossy without even knowing it! Wouldn't you like to know if you are ever being bossy? I know I would. This is definitely an important social skill to know.

Bossy kids might:

* Tell you what games you can play
* Tell you what to do in class
* Tell you how to think or what to say to others
* Tell you who you can play with and who you can't

Directions

Think of a person you know who is bossy. Draw how you feel when they boss you around. What feelings do you have? List them after your picture.

My Feelings

Now that you know how it feels to be bossed around, you can be extra aware when you might be doing it yourself. Being bossed around is not a fun feeling. If you are ever bossy, it might just be because you are afraid that you won't get your way, or that others won't listen to you unless you force yourself into the conversation. But while bossiness might get you your way today, it doesn't build healthy relationships.

Start to pay attention to when you might be sounding too bossy, so you can catch it right away. Maybe you can even stop bossiness in its tracks and say, "But that's just my opinion. What do *you* think?" The sooner we are aware of our behavior, the sooner we can fix it and get back on track to making great connections with others.

SPIDERWEB TALKS

You are really picking up some skills! Now you know how to start a conversation and how to keep it going. You even know how to stop bossiness in its tracks. But there is another key ingredient we haven't talked about yet—staying on topic.

When you are talking to someone, conversation flows more naturally when you stay on topic. That means you talk about the same things the other person is talking about.

For instance, if your friend is talking about tennis, you wouldn't suddenly start talking about football. That would make your friend feel that you weren't listening or that you didn't care about what they were saying.

It's okay to change topics; you just have to be a bit smooth about it.

For example, say your friend is talking about tennis and you want to talk about football. You can change topics by saying something like, "Tennis sounds like a great sport—I've never tried it. My favorite sport is football."

Do you see how you linked the topic "sports," but changed the theme to football?

Let's practice!

What you need

Someone in your family

Directions

Have a conversation with someone in your family. When they talk, have them write the question they ask you and draw a circle around it. When you respond and ask your question, do the same thing—write it down and circle it. Then draw a line connecting their circle to your circle. Go back and forth until you have a conversation spiderweb. Do you see how all the topics are interconnected? Conversations are more enjoyable when the topics are all linked.

Here's an example of how such a conversation would go:

DAD: *Did you have fun at school today?*

YOU: *I forgot my lunch money, but I got an A on my math test. (You think for a second.) Um, how was your day?*

DAD: *It was good. What did you eat for lunch?*

YOU: *The cafeteria gave me a cheese sandwich. (You think for a second.) What did you eat for lunch?*

DAD: *A salad. Your cheese sandwich sounds better. Did you finish your homework so you can watch the game tonight?*

YOU: *Yes, but can we watch a movie instead?*

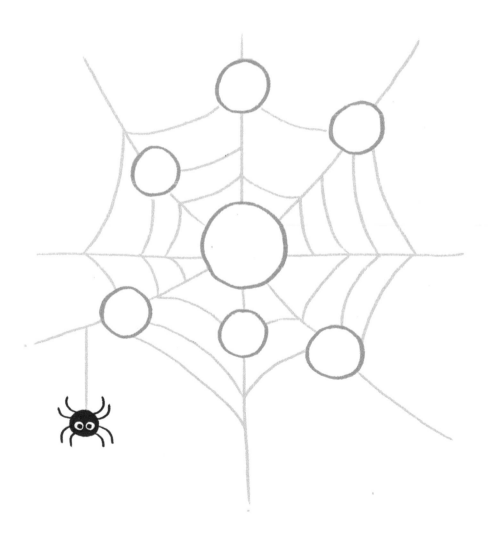

I'M INTERESTED! GIVING BODY LANGUAGE CLUES

When you're talking to someone, it's nice to show you are interested in what they say. Even if you don't care too much about what they're saying, it can be a good friend-maker to try to show some interest. But if you *love* what they are talking about but forget to show it, they'll think you don't care! And you don't want people to think you don't care, because that can be a friendship killer.

But wait—there are many ways to show someone you are interested in what they have to say. Here are just a few things you can do:

- Make eye contact
- Nod in agreement when they speak
- Change your expressions depending on what they are telling you
- Ask questions about what they are talking about
- Lean in just a bit
- Focus on the person talking
- Don't look at other people or things

Directions

Look at the picture on the next page. Can you spot the clues that show the girl is listening to her friend? Circle the clues and make a list of what you find.

BONUS ACTIVITY

How do you show others that you are listening? Pay attention to what types of clues you give. If you find you aren't giving enough clues, try adding a few of the things we talked about. Do you notice any changes? Does the speaker continue speaking or become more excited? If so, you're probably doing a great job showing you care.

TIME TO SAY GOODBYE—*ALREADY?*

Phew, we've covered a lot of social skills in just one chapter! Now it's time for us to say goodbye. No, the book isn't done—we're just going to learn how to say goodbye in a conversation. All good conversations must come to an end, but they don't have to end awkwardly.

Just as we had some good conversation starters, let's have some good conversation enders that we can have prepackaged and ready to use. Conversation enders are important because they help you leave the chat on a positive note. Good enders can leave people feeling that it was a good conversation and that you would like to talk again sometime.

Here are some examples of great ways to end a conversation:

Well, it was great talking to you.
I have to get back to [whatever you were doing before you started]. Let's talk again sometime.
We should get together sometime. We'll have to plan it. But I have to go.
I have to run, but it was nice talking to you.
I have to go. We should hang out again; it was cool talking to you.

Can you think of any others? List them here:

- -

- -

- -

- -

- -

- -

- -

BONUS ACTIVITY

· ·

Choose a conversation ender from the list or make up your own on the fly. The next time you're talking to someone, use one of your prepackaged conversation enders. How did the person respond? The more you practice using them, the easier ending a conversation will become.

TOP 10 TIPS FOR TALKING TO ADULTS

Talking to grown-ups is a little different from talking to kids. It's basically about respect. You'll recognize some of the tips from the skills you learned to talk to other kids, and there are new tips, too. These are great skills to practice with parents, grandparents, teachers, coaches, bus drivers, or any other grown-ups:

1. Make and keep eye contact.

2. Try to answer questions with more than just a "yes," or "no."

3. Show that you are interested by focusing on the conversation.

4. Throw back questions they asked you to show interest.

5. Be polite by using words like "thank you" and "you, too."

6. Speak up and don't mumble.

7. Don't interrupt—wait your turn to speak.

8. Don't talk disrespectfully.

9. If you disagree, do it in a polite way.

10. End the conversation with one of your conversation enders.

Why does it matter? Being respectful to grown-ups is the right thing to do, and it has many rewards. Today, it will help boost your reputation as a nice and polite kid; tomorrow, these skills may get you the job you want—so practice that firm handshake, too!

YOU CRACKED THE CODE!

You are well on your way to having some awesome social skills! In this chapter, you've already learned:

- How to start a conversation
- How to ask questions
- How to keep the conversation flowing
- How to not be too bossy or interrupt
- How to bounce questions back
- How to keep conversations on topic
- How to end a conversation

Feeling more confident? When you know the tricks to having a conversation, you have a huge skill under your belt. Once you master that, everything else will fall into place. Yep, you've just added some big superpower social skills.

Next, we'll move on to our listening skills. Being a good listener is one of the most important ingredients in being a friend. So listen up! I'm going to teach you what it takes to be a great listener.

Chapter Three

LISTEN UP!

We all have important things to say. But do you know what might be even more important than talking? Listening. There is nothing better than having a friend who is a great listener. Do you have someone who always listens to you? Maybe it's your mom or dad. Maybe it's a grandparent or a favorite aunt, uncle, or cousin. It can even be a pet! Do you have any pets at home? Do you sometimes talk to them? If not, you should! Even though our pets don't talk back, we can feel really close to them. Part of the reason for that is because they are happy to just sit there, be with you, and listen (and of course get their ears scratched).

We all want to be heard. We all want to feel that what we say is important to others. Being a good listener shows your friends, your parents, and everyone around you that you care.

But did you know that being a good listener isn't just about using our ears? We need to also use our eyes and our heart. Remember those other social skill superpowers we talked about at the beginning of the book? We want to make sure we are always using what we see, hear, and feel when interacting with others—even when we are just listening. This involves a little bit of intuition. Intuition is a little like mind-reading. We just need to use our senses to decide how someone is reacting to our words and our behaviors.

Sounds a little confusing right now, I know. But you'll see what I mean through the activities we'll do in this chapter.

BODY BUBBLES

We can make people uncomfortable with what we say to them. But we can also make people feel uncomfortable by how close we stand to them. When you are talking to someone, you want to be aware of how much space is between you and the other person. Have you ever felt weird when someone was standing way too close to you? Even if you're listening closely, *standing* too closely can ruin the whole conversation. To learn how close to stand, we can use body bubbles.

How much space is needed? Let's test it out.

What you need

A hula hoop or just your arm

Directions

Sometimes *seeing* what to do can be even better than *reading* what to do. Grab a hula hoop if you have one. Stand in the middle of the hula hoop and hold it up. This hula hoop represents your "body bubble." Normally, unless they are coming in for a hug, friends should stay out of your "body bubble." The space within the hula hoop is your private personal space. In a typical conversation, people shouldn't enter your body bubble, and you shouldn't enter other people's body bubbles.

If you don't have a hula hoop, you can use your arm. Stand in front of someone in your family. Extend your arm all the way out. This is called "arm's length." You want to normally be at about "arm's length" when talking and listening to friends. When talking and listening to your parents or siblings, you might get a little closer.

BONUS ACTIVITY

Go up to a family member and stand inside their body bubble while talking to them. Did they look uncomfortable? Did they take a step back to get you out of their body bubble? Did the conversation feel awkward?

It's important to learn the amount of space you should have between you and the person you're speaking and listening to. Pay attention to how close you stand to others. Now that you know about the body bubble, ask yourself, *Am I too close? Too far?* What about others? Does anyone get so close to you that you feel like saying, *This is a little too close?!*

PRACTICING PATIENCE

When we are having a great conversation, we might want to steer the conversation back to us and what *we* want to talk about. It is important to practice patience—to listen—when talking to others.

Have you ever played tag at recess? You know that it's not fun when you're always "it" and always the one chasing. A good balance makes the game fun. The same is true for conversations. It is important to learn how to balance a conversation. You want to balance how much you talk and how much you listen, how much of the conversation is about you and how much the conversation is about the other person. When we balance a conversation, we make sure that we listen. Let's practice here.

Directions

Here is a conversation Joe is having with his friend Rachel.

JOE: *I'm so excited for summer break!*

RACHEL: *Me too.*

JOE: *We are going to go to Texas to visit my grandma. I love visiting her. We have so much fun.*

RACHEL: *Cool.*

JOE: *We go hiking and swimming.*

RACHEL: *Neat.*

JOE: *We might go somewhere else too. Maybe Florida. My aunt lives there.*

RACHEL: *Oh.*

JOE: *There is tons to do in Florida. We love the beach.*

RACHEL: *Yeah, I love the beach, too.*

JOE: *My other aunt lives there, too. We visit her house tons. She has the cutest dog.*

RACHEL: *Awww.*

JOE: *Yeah, she's a Labrador Retriever. Her name is Molly. I love playing with her.*

Are you starting to see that this conversation is all about Joe? This is a one-sided conversation—Joe does not give Rachel a chance to speak about her trips or her family or anything else. Where do you think Joe should have stopped talking about himself? Draw a line where you think he could have turned the conversation to Rachel and listened to her.

What do you think Joe could have asked Rachel to let her start talking? Asking other people questions is a great way to show them that it is "their turn" in the conversation and that you are ready to listen.

Write a few questions Joe could have asked Rachel:

Nobody likes to be stuck in a conversation that's all about someone else. When we listen to other people share their feelings, experiences, and thoughts, they enjoy talking to us more!

BONUS ACTIVITY

The next time you are with your family or friends, do a social experiment. Practice listening and being patient as the other person talks. Ask the person at least one question about what *they* are talking about before you move the topic to yourself. Remember, people love to feel heard.

I GET IT!

To be a great listener, it's important to *actively* listen. This means you don't just sit there and stare at the person as they talk. Instead, you actively show that you are listening. You can do this by nodding, agreeing, and making eye contact. But an even better way to do it is to make related comments once in a while that show you are listening.

You can do this in a few different ways. You can:

- Comment about how that might make them feel

    Example: That must be so frustrating.

- Comment about how that would make you feel

    Example: I can only imagine. That would frustrate me!

- Ask them a question about what they did next

    Example: I can't believe she said that. What did you say after that?

Let's give this skill a whirl.

Directions

Read the following sentences. Write a comment you could make that would show you are actively listening.

EXAMPLE

I have been up all night studying and I still don't think I'll do well on the test!
Response: You must be exhausted.

NOW IT'S YOUR TURN!

The teacher called on me when I didn't know the answer. She's so mean!

Response:

- -

- -

She didn't invite me to her birthday party, but everyone else got an invitation.

Response:

- -

- -

Yesterday I was sick and now I am so behind on all my schoolwork.

Response:

- -

- -

I'm so excited! Tomorrow we go on our family trip!

Response:

- -

- -

BONUS ACTIVITY

Take your new skills out for a spin. Try showing your friends that you are listening by using one of the responses we talked about. Do they respond in a positive way? If so, nice work! If not, don't worry—it probably made them happy anyway.

ARE THEY INTERESTED? DECODING BODY LANGUAGE CLUES

We listen with our ears, but we can also listen with our heart. Have you ever looked at your pet and just knew that they were sad? Or looked across the playground and could tell someone was angry? How did you know that if they didn't say anything? It was most likely due to their body language. Just like that saying, "A picture is worth a thousand words," what we do with our body says tons about how we feel. That is why understanding body language—and actually listening to it—is so important when talking to people.

Some people may not tell you when they are bored, angry, or getting annoyed by you—but their body language might!

Let's see how good you are at decoding body language clues.

Directions

Answer the following questions. Check the key on page 50 to see if you were right.

EYES

1. Eyes—and eyebrows—tell us a lot about how someone is feeling. Can you guess what emotions go with each set of eyes and eyebrows? Write what emotion you think goes with each face.

ARMS

2. Arms can tell us how someone is feeling. Can you guess who is enjoying the conversation and who is not? Circle the picture of the person who is enjoying the conversation.

ARE THEY INTERESTED? DECODING BODY LANGUAGE CLUES, *continued*

BODY POSITION

3. How a person positions their body can tell you if they are interested in talking to you or not. Circle the picture of the person who is *not* interested in the conversation.

Answer Key

1A. Angry 1B. Surprised 1C. Sad 1D. Happy 2. B 3. B

BONUS ACTIVITY

Start paying attention to the body language clues people give you. You can even watch other people as they talk to each other. What can you detect people saying with just their body? The more you start noticing and listening to body language, the more you'll understand how people feel around you.

THE "SPREADING CARE" EXPERIMENT

One way to be an amazing listener is to show others you care. When you listen (with your ears, eyes, and heart, of course!), you learn what you can do to help. Being kind to others and doing considerate things tells the world that you are a caring person. When people experience your kindness or observe you being kind to others, they are likely to want to be with you more because you are a genuinely nice person.

There are so many ways to watch and listen, and then show you care. You can give someone an extra hand when they need it. You can notice when someone is sad or mad and ask them if they are okay—then, of course, listen to what they have to say. You can hold a door for someone behind you. The list can go on and on.

Directions

Answer the following questions.

What do people do to show they care about you?

- -

- -

- -

- -

How do you show other people you care about them?

- -

- -

- -

- -

THE "SPREADING CARE" EXPERIMENT, *continued*

BONUS ACTIVITY
· ·

Listen to what your family or friends are saying. What do they need? Do three things that show your friends or family that you care about them. Then write them here:

1. _____

_____

2. _____

_____

3. _____

_____

How did they respond? How did that make you feel? High-five—those are your social skill superpowers at work!

TOP 10 TIPS FOR A FUN CONVERSATION

Now that you know how to talk *and* listen, here are some tips to help make every conversation a positive one:

1. Ask the person questions about themselves.

2. Laugh and respond to the other person's jokes.

3. Share stories that make your point come alive.

4. Use examples when trying to explain something.

5. Roll with the punches, and try not to be too serious.

6. Relate to the person by saying things that let them know you "get" how they feel.

7. Use facial expressions that match the conversation.

8. Make sure your body language shows you are interested.

9. Don't make the conversation all about you and your interests.

10. Try not to be too argumentative. It's okay to "agree to disagree" (see "Let's Compromise," page 90) and leave it at that.

YOU CRACKED THE CODE!

You have added some really important superpowers to your social skills! Not only are you able to have a conversation with everyone and anyone, but you have also mastered the ability to be a good listener—with *all* your senses.

You now know that:

- Everyone has personal space that you should respect
- Conversations are about give and take, and patience is an awesome skill to master
- It's good to make comments that show you are listening
- Body language tells you a lot about what a person is thinking
- It's helpful to listen and show people you care

You have learned so much already, and we are about to get to the main meal! Chapters 1 through 3 are like appetizers. Now we are going to talk about the meat and potatoes of social skills: making and keeping friends.

In the next chapter, you'll learn:

- Why it is important to be a friend to *yourself*
- How to find friends
- How to keep friends
- How to survive difficult social situations
- How to understand friendship "rules"

Are you ready? Let's dig into that main dish!

Chapter Four

MAKING FRIENDS

In the first three chapters, you gathered many of the skills you need to make friends. You've learned what social skills are, and why they are so important. You've learned how to start and keep conversations going. You've learned how to be a great listener. These are all helpful ingredients to make friends. But now, we must mix all these ingredients together, along with a few extras, to get the outcome we are looking for—awesome friendships!

Let's get cookin'!

WORD SALAD

Did you know you can't be a friend to anyone else until you are a friend to yourself? It's true. You see, if you don't love yourself and treat yourself with kindness, it will be hard to expect other people to treat you that way. So let's spend a few activities focusing on making friends with the most important person in the world: you!

Let's explore what you think of yourself by making a "word salad."

Directions

How would you describe yourself? On the picture of the body, write lots of words that you think best describe you. Now, circle the positive/good ones, and count how many words are positive. Then put an X through the negative/bad ones, and count how many are negative. Were there more positive or negative words?

Now you're going to focus on the positive!

Take just the positive words, and write them down on a piece of paper. Tape the paper up in your bedroom. Can you add to the list? Whenever you think of another positive word to describe yourself, add it to the list. How big can you make this list grow in the next few weeks? Try reading the words out loud. Now, read it like you mean it! How is the list making you feel? Are you feeling more positive?

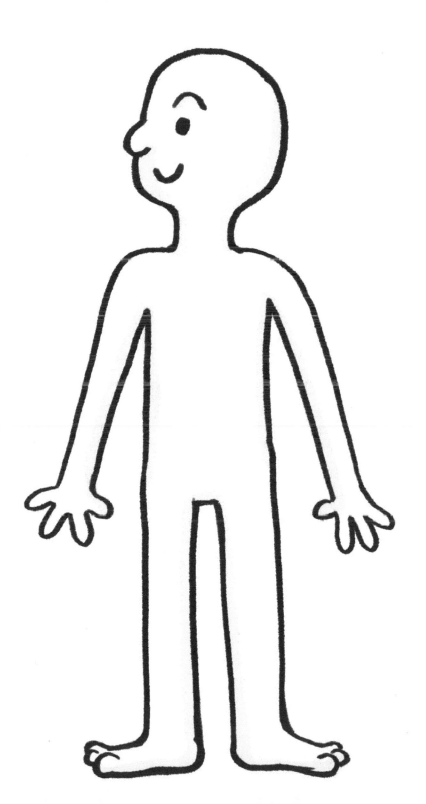

REFRAMING THOUGHT BUBBLES

We have tons of thoughts, right? And many of these thoughts are about what we say and do. Do you notice what you are thinking or telling yourself? Are these positive or negative messages? If you're always putting yourself down, this journey of making friends can be more challenging. To be happy and give off positive vibes, it's important to pump ourselves up, not tear ourselves down. What we tell ourselves can be motivating and encouraging or upsetting and discouraging. It's not bragging—you deserve to love yourself! In fact, you should be your own best cheerleader, and if you aren't there yet, there are things you can do to learn to feel more positive about yourself.

Which thoughts sound more like you? Circle the sentences that fit you better.

Yes! I did so well on that test!	I really messed up that test!
Everyone loves talking to me.	No one likes talking to me.
My hair looks really nice today.	My hair is a mess today.
I am so good at math.	I am the worst student in my class.
Everyone thinks I am so funny.	Everyone laughs at me.
I am really good at jump rope.	I am really clumsy.
I love how I can draw.	I can barely draw a stick figure.

What kind of thoughts do you have?

- -

- -

- -

Directions

Pay attention to your thoughts for one whole day. Come back and fill in the thought bubbles on the next page. What thoughts did you have? Were you being a nice or mean friend to yourself? If you found that you had some mean thoughts about yourself, try to rewrite those thoughts to be more positive. If you have trouble coming up with positive thoughts, ask yourself, *What would I say to a friend?*

After you complete this activity, think about your thoughts over the next few days. Are you having more positive thoughts—are you being a better friend to yourself? See if you can capture any negative thoughts in their tracks and "reframe" them into positives. For example, if you find yourself thinking, *I wish I were a better athlete,* tell yourself a positive truth—*I'm an awesome singer/speller/brother/sister*—whatever!

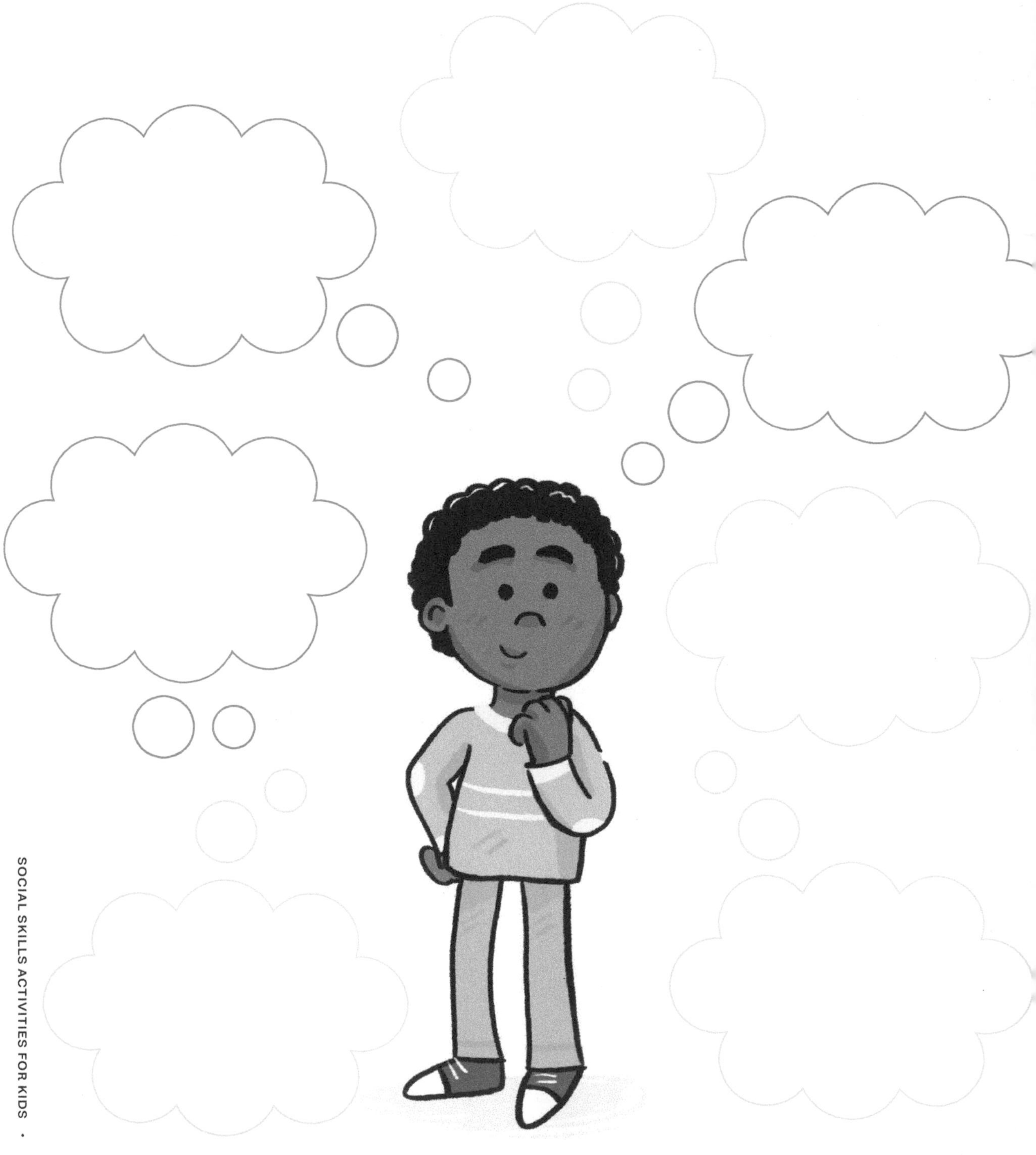

FINDING MY AWESOMENESS IN THREES

If you have no confidence or belief in yourself, of course it will be really hard for you to go up to people and try to become friends! Confidence is a big part of what makes us feel socially brave. When you are confident about how awesome you are, you will be less afraid of rejection from others.

Let's grow your awesomeness!

Directions

Draw a picture of yourself in the space below.

FINDING MY AWESOMENESS IN THREES, *continued*

Write three things you like about:

Your appearance (for example, *I like my smile.*)

- -

- -

- -

Your talents or skills (for example, *I am really good at soccer.*)

- -

- -

- -

Your personality (for example, *I am a very kind person.*)

- -

- -

- -

Do you remember how you wrote down the words to describe yourself in activity 21 (page 56)? Go check that list (hopefully it's still hanging up in your room) and add these positives to the list. Sometimes it's nice to be reminded of how awesome we truly are!

WHAT DO I TELL MYSELF?

Some of us are too afraid to make friends because of what we tell ourselves. If you beat yourself up by believing you are things like *too awkward*, or *too stupid, too nerdy*, you might think no one would want to be your friend.

Are there unhelpful things that you tell yourself?

Directions

Fill in any of the following blanks that you can relate to.

People wouldn't want to be friends with me because I'm _____.

I don't have friends because I'm way too _____.

People don't like me because _____.

If I could get rid of this about myself: _____, **I could make friends more easily.**

Did you fill one or more (or all) of those in? Give yourself a hug!

Okay, now what if we flip that all around?

Fill in the following blanks:

I *would* make a good friend because I'm _____.

People *like* me because _____.

People *would* want to be friends with me because _____.

More good things about me include _____.

Do you feel better? You should! You have positive, wonderful traits and you can see what some of them are. These will help you make and keep friends.

HOW DO OTHERS SEE ME?

Sometimes we can't see our good qualities as well as other people can. This activity will help you see how other people see you.

Ask several people you know and trust to list three words to describe you. Family members, trusted friends, and teachers are good choices. Answer the following questions.

What were the words most commonly used to describe you?

- -

- -

- -

Were the words you used to describe yourself (on page 56) different from the ones other people used to describe you? Were there any surprises? What were they?

- -

- -

- -

Did people use positive words to describe you?

- -

Look back at that ever-growing list you started in activity 21 (page 56). Are the words people used to describe you on that list? If not, it might be a good idea to add them. That way, when you are having a bad day or are feeling blue about yourself, you can read this list and remind yourself of the awesome person that you are!

WHAT INGREDIENTS ARE IN A FRIEND?

We all have likes and dislikes. Some people love salty foods, while others have more of a sweet tooth. Friends come in all sorts of "flavors" and varieties, too. Some are loud and outgoing, and others are quiet and shy. Before trying to make a friend, it can help to know what kind of "friend ingredients" you prefer.

Trying to make bread without knowing the ingredients would be a disaster. You might make a great effort to bake a loaf of bread, only to find that your bread falls flat. Making friends can take some effort, too, and you want your effort to pay off with a friendship you'll really enjoy.

Luckily, when you know what type of ingredients you are looking for, it makes finding a friend that much easier.

So let's line up our ingredients.

What ingredients are you looking for in a friend? Go through this "shopping list" and check off all the qualities you would like in a friend. Add your own special ingredients at the bottom.

❏ Friendly	❏ Talkative	❏ Has lots of friends
❏ Shy	❏ Quiet	❏ Doesn't have many friends
❏ Smart	❏ Likes to play an instrument	❏ Likes to do art
❏ Loud	❏ Silly	❏ Serious
❏ Likes to read	❏ Plays computer games	❏ Plays sports
❏ Trustworthy	❏ Can keep a secret	❏ Stands up for people
❏ Kind	❏ Helpful	❏ Brave
Fill in:	Fill in:	Fill in:

Remember that while you may look for certain qualities in a friend, just about anyone can be a friend. If you open yourself up as a friendly person, you may find friends who don't match up to your usual "requirements." The important thing is to find friends who are kind, make you feel good, and are fun to be with.

MAP IT OUT!

Now that we know what type of ingredients are in a good friend, let's figure out where to look for them. We can find friends in the most unlikely places. Where can you make friends? Are there kids you know who could turn into friends?

Let's map it out.

Directions

Fill in the islands on the map on the next page with all the places you can possibly meet friends. If you know of a particular person you want to try to be friends with, write their name on the map, too. Here's a list to get you started:

- Class
- Lunch
- Recess
- Neighborhood
- Church/synagogue/mosque/place of worship
- Sports/extracurricular activities
- Relatives/cousins (they count, too!)

DOS AND DON'TS FOR MAKING FRIENDS

When we are trying to make friends, there are things we can do that will really help us—and there are things we can do that will really hurt us. Sometimes kids don't know what those things are, and they may get confused when making friends doesn't go well.

To help you out, I thought we could go over some basic rules for making friends. Here's a list of Dos and Don'ts when trying to start a friendship.

Directions

Read the following list. Can you think of some Dos and Don'ts to add? Write them at the bottom of the list.

The Dos and Don'ts for Making Friends

DO . . .	DON'T . . .
Ask someone if they want to be your friend.	Interrupt a conversation to introduce yourself.
Ask someone if you can have their phone number.	Call or text their number over and over again.
Call or text someone to invite them over.	Call or text a friend late at night or early in the morning.
Ask to join in and play with a group.	Talk meanly about other kids.

DO . . .	DON'T . . .
Take turns playing what each friend wants to play.	Insist that everyone play your game and play it your way.
Fill in:	Fill in:
Fill in:	Fill in:
Fill in:	Fill in:

Can you think of a time when a friend did something from the Do list or the Don't list?

- -

Describe a time when someone did something from the Do list. How did that make you feel? Why?

- -

- -

- -

Describe a time when someone did something from the Don't list. How did that make you feel? Why?

- -

- -

- -

DOUBLE DUTCH

Have you ever played Double Dutch jump rope? It's when two jump ropes are being swung at the same time and you have to jump into them. The whole idea seemed too scary for me as a kid, but some kids are really good at it.

Jumping into a group can feel the same way. It can seem really hard and even a bit scary. You might think, *What if they laugh at me? What if they ignore me?* Or even worse: *What if they are mean to me?*

Trying to join a group can take courage and planning. What can you say or do to join a group?

Here is a list of possible things to say:

- What are you guys doing?
- What are you guys playing?
- Can I play, too?
- Can I join you?

You can also just jump into the conversation. Here are some examples of what that might sound like:

- I also heard that song
- That was so funny—I saw that, too
- I play that as well

You can even join a group with just your body language. Here are some examples of what that might look like:

- Nodding your head
- Smiling
- Laughing with the group

Let's practice how it would feel to jump into a conversation. On the next page are three situations where a group is talking. Mark would like to join in. Write down a way that Mark can join the group. If you need help, look at the lists above.

CONVERSATION #1

TALI: *I love that restaurant! My family goes there all the time.*

BRODY: *Me, too!*

SAM: *We went there for my birthday last month. It was so good.*

Mark is sitting right next to the group. What can he say to join in?

- -

CONVERSATION #2

TALI: *That was the best movie ever!*

BRODY: *I think that was my favorite movie, too.*

SAM: *I didn't get to see it yet.*

Mark is sitting at the table with the group. What can he say to join in?

- -

CONVERSATION #3

TALI: *We just got a new dog. He is so cute!*

BRODY: *What kind is it?*

TALI: *He's a poodle.*

SAM: *Awww! I love poodles.*

Mark is standing with the group. What can he say to join in?

- -

Was it easy to come up with ways to help Mark join in? Remember, the more you practice, the easier it will become.

DOUBLE DUTCH, *continued*

BONUS ACTIVITY

· ·

Find a group chatting at school and join in. Use one of the suggested phrases
or try adding to the conversation by relating to something that was said. How
did it go?

TOP 10 THINGS TO SAY TO A NEW FRIEND

1. My name is _____. What's your name?

2. Do you want to play?

3. What do you want to play?

4. What things do you like to do for fun?

5. Would you like to come over some time?

6. Do you have any pets?

7. What's your favorite TV show?

8. Do you have brothers or sisters?

9. Do you live near me?

10. How old are you?

YOU CRACKED THE CODE!

We covered tons in this chapter! I hope you now see that being friends with *yourself* is one of the most important things you can do to build your social skills. When you feel good about yourself, your confidence will help you make friends with others. To build your confidence, you learned:

- What you like about yourself
- What makes you unique and awesome
- What beliefs hold you back from making friends
- What qualities you look for in a friend
- What to do and what not to do to make friends
- How to jump into a conversation

Now that you know how to make friends, in the next chapter I'll show you how to keep them. You'll learn:

- How to tell if you are being overly sensitive
- The Dos and Don'ts of keeping friends
- How to handle gossip
- How to handle disagreements
- What to do when your friends make poor decisions
- How to stand up for what you believe in

After the next chapter you will be an old pro at making and keeping friends!

Chapter Five

KEEPING FRIENDS

Once you make friends, your job isn't finished—you want to keep the friendships you made. Sometimes that can get tricky. Friends can have disagreements, gossip, and even hurt your feelings from time to time.

In this chapter you'll learn how to deal with all the curveballs friendship can throw your way, while keeping the good friendships you've made.

HOW SENSITIVE AM I?

We all get our feelings hurt. People sometimes say or do things that make us feel sad, embarrassed, or angry. But some of us get our feelings hurt really easily, and some of us don't. What that means is that some of us are really sensitive, and some of us aren't.

When we are very sensitive, we might feel like our friends are being mean even when they aren't. We might feel like people don't want to play with us, even when they do. Knowing how sensitive you are will help you know when to dial down, or chill, your reactions to what your friends do or say.

How sensitive are you to what people say or do?

Let's find out!

Directions

Put a check mark next to the situations that would make you feel hurt, embarrassed, or upset. Don't check the sentence if you don't think the situation would bother you. At the end, count how many sentences you checked, and see your sensitivity score.

❏ Your friend is sitting with you at lunch. They turn around and start talking to another friend the whole lunch period.

❏ Your teacher calls out your name and says sternly to you, "Stop messing around and pay attention!"

❏ Your friends don't let you pick any of the games to play at recess.

❏ Everyone in class has to get a partner. No one asks to partner up with you.

❏ When playing tag, the other kids always make you be "it."

❏ You find out that two of your friends went to the movies over the weekend without you.

❏ A kid you aren't friends with invites other people to their birthday party, but not you.

❏ You say "hi" to your friend, but they look distracted and don't say "hi" back.

❏ You call a friend to hang out, and they don't call you back or respond for three hours.

❏ You ask a friend to come over to play, but they say they are busy.

❏ You get a haircut, and no one says anything about it.

❏ Everyone is doing a school project. Your friend says yours looks too big.

❏ Halfway through the school day, someone tells you that your T-shirt is on backward.

❏ You are laughing loudly with your friends, and another kid in your class asks you to be quiet.

❏ You get in the wrong line at lunch, and the lunch lady shouts for you to go to the other line.

❏ You have a friend over, and your mom yells at you to clean your room.

❏ Your friend comments that you wore the same shirt two days in a row.

❏ You try to talk to a new student, but they just stare at you.

❏ You are talking to your best friend about your favorite video game and they look bored.

❏ Your teacher picks a "Star Student" every week, and it has been four months and you haven't been picked yet.

Count up how many checks you have, and see where you rate in sensitivity:

0–10 checks You are probably not that sensitive. You can let many things go and your feelings don't get hurt too easily.

10–15 checks You are a bit more sensitive. Things might upset you more often than other kids.

15–20 checks You are very sensitive. Your feelings might get hurt much more easily than other kids.

HOW SENSITIVE AM I?, *continued*

Where did you rate? If you rated "more" or "very" sensitive, don't worry about it. I got a 20 out of 20! Sensitive people are also some of the most kindhearted people on this planet. So although your feelings might get hurt more often, you are also more likely to notice when other people's feelings get hurt, too—and that can be a social skill superpower in itself! Check out the bonus activity in the box to learn how you can stay positive when your feelings get hurt.

BONUS ACTIVITY

The next time you feel yourself hurt by something someone does or says, ask yourself these questions:

- Was their comment directed at me?
- Are they having a bad day?
- Am I assuming something that they didn't really say or do?
- Did they do it to other people, too?
- Are they normally like that or is it just today?
- Could there be something else going on that I don't know about?

Sometimes when we take a step back and look at a situation with fresh eyes, we can see a situation differently. I know I've made many wrong assumptions when I didn't take a step back!

COMMON SOCIAL RULES VS. SENSITIVE RULES

When we are a bit more sensitive, we tend to have different social rules than other people. We might think others should act or behave in ways that aren't always realistic. We might think that people should be as polite or kind as we are to them. It's important for us to realize that not everyone will treat us the same way we treat them. And although that might be disappointing, those people are not actually breaking any social rules.

For example, some sensitive people might get hurt if their friend talks to other people. You might feel like your friends should be loyal only to you. Having sensitive rules can be a problem, because many other people don't follow them. That can lead us to getting hurt over and over again. This is why it's helpful to swap out our "sensitive rules" (the rules for the way we think people should act) for the "common social rules" (more realistic rules). That doesn't mean you have to change your own awesome behavior—it just means you probably shouldn't expect everyone to act the same as you.

Let's explore the difference between a common rule and a sensitive rule.

Directions

Read the sentences below. Put a "C" next to the rules that sound like a common social rule and an "S" next to the rules that sound like a sensitive rule that might need to be changed.

___1. If you are my best friend, you cannot have any other best friends.

___2. My best friend doesn't always have to play with me.

___3. If I call someone, they don't have to call me back right away.

___4. If I invite someone over, they should invite me over next.

___5. If I give someone a compliment, they should give me a compliment back.

___6. If I help a friend, they owe me one.

KEEPING FRIENDS ·

COMMON SOCIAL RULES VS. SENSITIVE RULES, *continued*

___7. If I do someone a favor, they don't owe me anything.

___8. If someone calls me, I don't have to call them back right away.

___9. If I am playing with a friend at recess, they shouldn't let anyone else join in.

___10. If I sit with someone at lunch, it is okay if they invite someone else to sit with us.

How did you answer? If you put an S next to numbers 1, 4, 5, 6, 9 (or most of them), you probably have a pretty good idea of the difference between sensitive and common social rules, and hopefully you can try to relax your expectations a bit—this will keep friendships running smoothly and help you avoid conflict. Number 4 is tricky, because while it's important to have give and take in a friendship, not everyone is able to have people over to their house (or be comfortable doing so). It shouldn't be a friendship deal breaker.

Do you have some sensitive rules?

If so, write down a list of things that bother you, or social rules that you think might be too sensitive. Talk to a parent, friend, or relative, and share your list. Ask them how they feel about your social rules. Did they think some of them were too sensitive? Asking friends and relatives their thoughts about a particular situation is a great way to know if you need to turn down the sensitivity dial or not. Below, rewrite the sensitive rules and trade them for common social rules that you can believe in.

For example:

- *Sensitive Rule:* My best friend shouldn't have play dates with any other kids.
- *Changed to a Common Social Rule:* My best friend can have play dates with other kids. It doesn't mean that we aren't best friends anymore

Review this list when a situation pops up and you aren't sure if you are being too sensitive.

Sensitive Rule:

- -

Common Social Rule:

- -

Sensitive Rule:

- -

Common Social Rule:

- -

Sensitive Rule:

- -

Common Social Rule:

- -

WHEN THREE'S A CROWD

Even though it's nice to have many friends, sometimes having lots of friends can be hard. What if your friends don't like each other? What if you want to play with different people each day? What if you want to talk to one person, but you don't want to leave out another?

Learning how to handle more than one friend at a time is an important social skill.

Directions

Here are some tricky social situations involving more than one friend. Pick the best way to handle each situation. When you are done, check the answer key at the bottom.

1. You want to play with two of your friends, but they don't want to play with each other. You:
    a. Tell them that if they don't play with each other, you won't play with either of them.
    b. Tell them you'll take turns playing with one of them each day at recess.
    c. Run away and cry.

2. You are sitting with a few friends. You notice that one friend isn't talking at all. You:
    a. Ignore your quiet friend and keep talking.
    b. Give your quiet friend an angry glare and keep talking.
    c. Ask your quiet friend a question to get him involved in the conversation.

3. Your friend gives you a birthday invitation but doesn't invite your other friend. You:
    a. Tell your friend that you are sorry she is not invited and brag that you are going.
    b. Don't discuss the party in front of your other friend.
    c. Give back the birthday invitation and say you can't go if your other friend isn't invited.

Answer Key

1. B 2. C 3. B

If you answered all these questions correctly, you've got a good handle on how to handle multiple friends. And remember, nobody can tell you who you can or can't be friends with—not even your friends. *You* get to choose!

THE FRIEND PLAYBOOK

Just like there are Dos and Don'ts for *making* friends, there are Dos and Don'ts for *keeping* friends. So what's in the friend playbook? Let's have a look at some of the social "rules."

Directions

Read the following list, then follow the directions.

DO . . .	DON'T . . .
When disagreeing with a friend, just "agree to disagree" and move on.	When disagreeing with a friend, insist that you are right and they are wrong.
Encourage other people to play with you and your friends.	Exclude other people and don't let your friends play with other people either.
Talk nicely about others or don't say anything at all.	Gossip and point out what you don't like about other kids.
Invite several friends over to your house.	Invite only one person over to your house in front of other kids.
Invite someone over for a play date.	Invite yourself over to someone else's house for a play date.
Take turns when playing or sharing something.	Don't share anything you have and refuse to take turns.

KEEPING FRIENDS · **85**

THE FRIEND PLAYBOOK, *continued*

In the space below, draw how you felt when someone did something from the Don't column:

TOP 10 TIPS FOR BEING A GOOD FRIEND

The best kinds of friends are those you can count on. They are always kind—not just to their friends, but to everyone. Check out this list of tips for being the sort of person others will want to be friends with.

1. Be kind and thoughtful.

2. Be helpful and offer to do things for your friends.

3. Agree to disagree when you don't see things the same way.

4. Take turns and be patient.

5. Be flexible and go with the flow.

6. Be aware of how your words and actions make people feel.

7. Don't gossip about other people.

8. Don't leave friends out.

9. Treat everyone with respect.

10. Don't talk only about what you like; listen and talk about what your friends like, too.

DID YOU HEAR?

Once you have a group of friends, social situations will come up that can be tricky. Gossip is definitely one of them. It's good to learn how to handle gossip, since it tends to be a common way that people can hurt feelings, damage friendships, and even cause big fights.

One way to know how to handle gossip is to ask yourself these two questions:

1. Would I want other people talking about me this way?

2. Could we say this in front of the person we are talking about?

If the answer is no to both, you might want to find a way to remove yourself from the conversation. Going to the bathroom or finding another way to excuse yourself from the conversation is a great ninja trick!

Directions

Below are some stories where gossip has gotten in the way of friendship. Think about the two rules I talked about, and decide how you would handle these situations. Look at the answer key on the next page to see if you were right.

1. You are friends with Susan and Sarah, but Susan and Sarah don't like each other. Sarah comes over to you and says she heard that Susan picks her nose. You:
   a. Say, "Ooh that's gross!"
   b. Say, "I don't want to talk about Susan, she's my friend."
   c. Walk right over to Susan and tell her what Sarah said.

2. Jack comes up to you at lunch and says he heard that Todd, another kid in your class, is in love with Kayla. You:
   a. Go up to Kayla and tell her that Todd likes her.
   b. Argue with Jack that what he is saying isn't true.
   c. Tell Jack that it isn't your business and then change the subject.

3. Karen and Carrie are in a big fight. Neither of them are good friends with you. Carrie comes over and tells you that Karen has always hated you and that you shouldn't like her. You:

   a. Tell Carrie that you don't want to get in the middle of their fight.

   b. Go up to Karen and ask her why she hates you.

   c. Tell Carrie that you should form an "I hate Karen" club.

4. Your friend Malik comes up to you and tells you that Jake, another kid in your class, wets the bed. He said he has proof because he once slept over at his house. You:

   a. Tell Malik that it's none of your business and then change the subject.

   b. Laugh and then make fun of Jake.

   c. Go whisper to all the other kids in the class that you know Jake wets the bed.

Answer Key

1. B 2. C 3. A 4. A

If you answered all these correctly, you are rocking the social skill superpowers. If not, look back at those two questions I asked earlier: How would you feel if you were the victim of gossip, and could you say these things in front of that person? Luckily, you can avoid gossip by simply stopping it in its tracks, as shown in these stories.

LET'S COMPROMISE!

Besides gossiping, constant fighting is another thing that can destroy friendships. Friends fight for all sorts of reasons, but learning how to compromise, problem-solve, and disagree in a respectful way is a superpower that you will want to grow.

There are three important steps you can take when disagreeing with a friend:

Step 1. Let the other person know you understand what they are saying.

Step 2. Explain your point or position.

Step 3. Offer a compromise as a solution.

Compromising means giving in just a little to offer a solution that pleases everyone. Let's see a few examples of what this would look like:

EXAMPLE 1

Kelly and Raquel are arguing because Kelly wants to eat lunch outside by the bench and Raquel wants to eat in the lunchroom.

Kelly says to Raquel:

Step 1

I know you like eating inside. *(letting her know she understands her)*

Step 2

But I really like to sit next to other friends, too, and they sit outside. *(explaining her point)*

Step 3

How about we take turns eating where each of us wants? *(offering a compromise)*

EXAMPLE 2

Norman and Mia are fighting because they both think they are the fastest runner in the class.

Norman says to Mia:

Step 1
You think you are the fastest runner. *(letting her know he understands her)*

Step 2
I think I am the fastest runner. *(explaining his point)*

Step 3
We are both good runners. Maybe we can just agree to disagree on who is the fastest runner. *(offering a compromise)*

EXAMPLE 3

Madeline feels like Latitia doesn't pay enough attention to her. She is upset that Latitia is always talking to other people.

Latitia says to Madeline:

Step 1
You feel like I don't pay enough attention to you. *(letting her know she understands her)*

Step 2
I really enjoy hanging out with you, but I also want to talk to my other friends. *(explaining her point)*

Step 3
Next time I am talking with them, I will try to include you more in our conversation. *(offering a compromise)*

Now it's your turn!

LET'S COMPROMISE!, *continued*

Directions

Here is a situation in which friends are disagreeing. Fill in what Emily should say for each step.

Aubrey is annoyed because Emily won't let her borrow one of her sparkly pencils. Emily doesn't want Aubrey to use her sparkly pencil because her grandma gave them to her and they are special. She is willing to let Aubrey borrow her rainbow pencil, though.

Fill in what Emily should say using our three-step process:

Step 1 *(letting her know she understands)*:

Step 2 *(explaining her point)*:

Step 3 *(offering a compromise)*:

BUT WE'RE ALL DOING IT!

Sometimes when we have friends, we do things with them that we might never do if we were on our own. We might make bad choices if everyone else is making bad choices. We might be mean if everyone else is being mean. We might break rules if everyone else is breaking rules.

But when you have friends, it doesn't mean you have to be a follower! It is really important to make sure that you stay true to yourself and don't change who you are to fit in with other people.

So how are you supposed to make better choices? You'll be surprised at how often people will follow *you* when you choose not to follow others. This is what being a leader is all about. It just takes one brave person to stand up for what they believe in. Other kids might be feeling uncomfortable as well but are too nervous to go against the crowd.

If you are ever in this type of situation and are worried about sticking out like a sore thumb and feeling awkward, there are some ninja moves you can do to get out of the situation.

Here are a few:

BAD SITUATION	NINJA MOVE
Your friends are riding bikes without wearing their helmets and they want you to, too.	You tell them your mom won't let you. (I let my kids use me as an excuse when they feel pressured by friends—maybe you can talk to your parents about this, too.)
Your friends are sharing the answers to a test.	You don't focus on them; you just keep your attention on your paper.
Your friends are talking bad about each other.	You say you have to go to the bathroom and leave the conversation.

BUT WE'RE ALL DOING IT!, *continued*

Have you ever been in a situation where your friends were making bad choices? How did you react? Did you do the right thing? If not, how could you have reacted differently?

Directions

Think of a time when you were with friends or other kids who were making bad choices. Fill in the answers:

The kids around me were making a bad choice by:

- -

- -

- -

- -

My reaction was to:

If I could do it over again I would:

The next time my friends or other kids around me make a bad choice, I am going to:

WHAT DO I STAND FOR?

Part of making and keeping friends is finding people who are similar to you—not in how they look, but in what activities they enjoy and what values they believe in.

Do you know what a *value* is? It is something that is important to you—not a thing, but a character trait or type of behavior. For instance, you might value being honest, or you might value someone who is thoughtful. You might value respecting others no matter what culture they come from.

Your friends won't always have the same values as you. So it's important to know what you are willing to stand up for—even if your friends feel differently. This will help *you* be *you*, even among a sea of friends. And people tend to respect other people who are willing to stand up for what they believe is right.

What matters to you? What would you stand up for, no matter what?

Directions

Here is a sample of values that people believe in. Put a check mark next to the ones that matter to you. Come up with three of your own at the end of the list.

Things That Matter to Me

❏ I want to talk to everyone in a nice voice.	❏ It is important to me that animals and insects are treated nicely.	❏ I like to treat everyone fairly.
❏ I don't like to spread gossip and say bad things about other people.	❏ I like to include everyone.	❏ I like to make sure that everyone feels happy.
❏ I am an honest person and I always tell the truth.	❏ I like to help those around me.	❏ I like to make sure everyone gets a turn.

❏ Even if I don't like someone, I am not mean to them.	❏ I like people regardless of the color of their skin.	❏ I like people regardless of their religion.
❏ I like people regardless of their weight.	❏ I am not a bully and I don't join in on bullying.	❏ I am a hard worker and do all my schoolwork.
Fill in:	Fill in:	Fill in:

Now look over your choices. Which things matter to you? The items you chose are the values that matter to you, so remember this: A good friend will never expect you to compromise or toss away your values. If you have friends who don't share your values, stick to them anyway because they are some of your most important strengths. Values are leadership skills, and they make us unique!

TO TELL OR NOT TO TELL?

No one likes tattletales, or kids who tell on others for every little thing. No one likes to get in trouble, and no one likes someone who gets them into trouble constantly. But when should you tell and when should you mind your own business? Deciding when to tell and when to not tell can be hard.

Here are some quick tips to decide if you should tell or not:

TELL	DON'T TELL
When someone is doing something dangerous	When it is not dangerous behavior
When someone is being bullied	When no one is being bullied
When someone can get hurt	When no one is getting hurt
When you told the person to stop and they are ignoring you	When you tell the person to stop and they listen

Directions

Here are different situations you might experience. Put a check mark next to what you would do in each situation.

SOCIAL SKILL	TELL	DON'T TELL
A boy in your class is saying he is going to beat up another boy after school.		
A girl is cheating on a test with another girl sitting in front of you.		
A kid cut in front of another kid at lunch.		
A boy is leaning too far back in his chair even though you told him he might fall.		
Kids in class are sneaking candy from the teacher's desk.		
Kids on the playground are kicking the new kid.		

TO TELL OR NOT TO TELL?, *continued*

Why did you put the answers you did? Did they fall into the Tell or Don't Tell categories I talked about? Some of these questions were hard to decide on, right? Next, go over your answers with an adult in your home. What did they think of your choices?

YOU CRACKED THE CODE!

Wow! You've done some great work. You really rolled up your sleeves and learned step-by-step what it takes to be an awesome friend. In this chapter, you learned:

- How to know when you are being extra sensitive and how to handle it
- How to play with more than one friend at a time
- How to handle gossip
- What to do when your friends aren't making the best choices
- How to handle the tricky parts of friendships

But we still have a few more things to explore! In the next chapter, we will take things one step further. You'll learn:

- Some common rules for school behavior
- How to ask questions in class
- How to talk to teachers and other grown-ups
- How to cooperate and be a good sport
- How to spread kindness to others

Your superpowers are almost fully charged up. Now let's super-charge you!

Chapter Six

IN SCHOOL AND OUT OF SCHOOL

Of course, there's more to social skills than just making friends. You are using your social skills when you interact with adults, talk to teachers, call to order a pizza, and even play a sport. Almost everything we do involves our social skills, so why not make social situations easy and even fun?

We have been working hard to build your social skill superpowers, and now we are going to grow your social skills far beyond friendships. We're going to talk about social skills and expectations in school and well beyond.

Are you ready? Let's dig in.

I SPY WITH MY LITTLE EYE

When you're in the classroom, there are certain social expectations you are supposed to follow. "Expectations" are the way you are supposed to behave in a situation. For instance, if you go to the movie theater, the social expectation is for you to sit quietly while watching the movie. To *not* do this would be breaking a social rule or expectation.

There are also expectations in the classroom. Your teacher has probably talked about what some of them are, maybe back at the beginning of the school year.

Here are just a few:

- Listen quietly and raise your hand before you speak
- Pay attention to the teacher
- Don't look at other people's answer
- Cover your mouth when you cough or sneeze
- Say "thank you" and "please" when talking to other students
- Give other students a turn to answer the teacher's questions
- When working as a group, listen to other people's ideas
- Keep your hands to yourself

Can you think of any others? Each class may have different social expectations, depending on the teacher, the class, and your age. Add three more social expectations from your class here:

- -

- -

- -

Directions

Here is a picture of a classroom out of control. Can you spot the kids breaking the social expectations in the class? Let's play I Spy. When you spy someone breaking a social expectation, circle it. I'll give you a hint—there are four students breaking social expectations.

I SPY WITH MY LITTLE EYE, *continued*

When we break social expectations in the classroom, we can rub our classmates the wrong way. Many kids don't want to be friends with someone who is loud, disrespectful, or inconsiderate. Learning how to follow social expectations can show others that you know how to behave and respect others. That's a great quality that people look for in a friend!

I DOUBLE DARE YOU!

When I was a kid, I used to be terrified of my friend's father. The funny part was, he was a nice man and always had a smile on his face, but grown-ups in general just freaked me out. I would do all I could to avoid going over to my friend's house, especially when I knew his dad was home.

With just a little bit of practice, I could have gotten over my fear. The more we avoid doing something, the bigger our fear grows. Practice makes perfect, and talking to grown-ups is something that we can practice and even get really good at.

That's right: Social skills aren't just about talking to other kids. It is super helpful to build your confidence when talking to teachers and other adults. Sometimes that means we have to do things that make us a little bit uncomfortable. Leaving your comfort zone can be hard, but with practice it can become no big deal at all!

Are you ready for a dare?

Directions

Here are nine different dares. Copy them onto small pieces of paper, fold each one, and put them in a bowl. Close your eyes and pick out one dare from the bowl. If you're up for the challenge, complete your dare for the day. Feeling even more daring? Do one dare every day for a week! The more dares you do, the easier they will become. When we get used to talking to adults, it won't feel like a big deal anymore.

Have your own dare ideas? Awesome! Add them to the collection.

Raise your hand and ask a question.	Go up to a teacher after class and ask a question.	Ask a grown-up you know how their day is going.
Ask a teacher if they have any pets.	Ask a teacher what their favorite color is.	Volunteer to help a teacher with a task or activity.
Say good morning to your bus driver or teacher.	Talk to one of the cafeteria workers.	Talk to one of the recess monitors or aides.
Fill in:	Fill in:	Fill in:

I DOUBLE DARE YOU!, *continued*

After you practice talking to grown-ups for a while, you'll be able to do it without much thought. Continue to grow your skills so you can get comfortable asking a teacher to repeat something you didn't understand, or even confiding in a trusted adult if you are having school or social troubles—grown-ups can be a big help!

CONNECT THE DOTS

People prefer to be friends with other people who are supportive and cooperative. Sometimes things don't go the way we want them to go, but it's important to handle situations without losing our cool. When kids don't take turns, are a bad sport, or only want to play if they win, other kids eventually won't want to play with them. We don't want that to happen to you!

Directions

Tommy isn't being a good sport and he is definitely *not* being cooperative! Jack is playing nicely with his friends—he is a good sport and cooperative. Below is a list of behaviors. Some are cooperative, and some are not. Can you draw a line between Tommy and Tommy's behaviors (not cooperative) and Jack and Jack's behaviors (cooperative)?

- He won't share the ball
- He passes the ball back and forth
- He lost, but said, "Good game"
- He insists that they play only *his* game at recess
- He made fun of a girl for missing the ball
- He got angry and tossed the ball over the fence
- He lost and shouted, "It's not fair!"
- He threw a ball at someone after he lost
- He volunteered to go get the ball when it went over a fence
- He suggested they take turns so everyone gets a chance to play

BONUS ACTIVITY

Now that you have a good idea of what is cooperative play and what is not, pay attention to your behavior the next time you're playing with others. Ask yourself, *Am I being a good sport?* and, *Am I being cooperative with everyone?* If the answer to either question is no, take a deep breath and turn your behavior around. These skills take practice and will improve over time, but catching them is the first step.

RANDOM ACTS OF KINDNESS

Being kind is one of the best ways to make friends. Kindness is a wonderful behavior, and most people are drawn to people who are nice. Being kind can come naturally, but we can always develop this skill.

Random acts of kindness are when you do something super kind for no reason at all. You can do random acts of kindness for friends, teachers, or even kids you don't know. It feels good to be nice, but it also sends a signal to others that you are a thoughtful, kind-hearted friend.

Here are a few ideas on how to show random acts of kindness:

- Hold the door for someone
- Go up to someone who is alone and ask them to play with you
- Ask someone how their day is going
- Offer to help another student in the classroom
- Teach a friend something they have a hard time doing
- Ask the teacher if there is anything extra you can do to help them
- Write a note to someone and tell them why they are awesome
- Slip a note to one of your favorite friends and tell them what you like about them

There are endless things you can do to be kind, "just because!" Can you think of some that you can do?

- -

- -

- -

- -

BONUS ACTIVITY

· ·

Pick from the previous examples or create your own random act of kindness and do it for someone. How did it feel? How did the other person respond?

    When we do kind things, not only does it feel good, but other people begin to appreciate us more, too!

WHO, WHAT, WHEN?

We've talked about expectations for how kids are supposed to act in the classroom. There are also expectations when it comes to asking questions.

Directions

Below is a quick quiz that tests your social skills about asking questions. Circle whether you think each statement is True or False.

You should:

1. Shout out answers if you know them. *True False*

2. Raise your hand and ask the teacher to explain something you don't understand. *True False*

3. Laugh when someone asks a simple question. *True False*

4. Give other kids a chance to ask questions. *True False*

5. Whisper your questions to kids sitting near you. *True False*

Answer Key

1. F 2. T 3. F 4. T 5. F

WHO, WHAT, WHEN?, *continued*

How'd you do? If you missed some, don't worry—just talk with a grown-up about your answers. They can help you understand more about the right way to behave, and why behaving correctly matters.

BONUS ACTIVITY

The next time you're in class, pay attention to how others around you ask questions. Do you see kids shouting out? Do you see some kids confused but not speaking up? What other things do you notice? Once you start to pay attention to the way others ask questions and behave, your own behavior is likely to start changing as well.

When we follow social rules like these, we send a message to others that we are respectful and not afraid to speak up if we need help. Both are important social skills!

TOP 10 TIPS FOR SOCIAL MEDIA

Social skills are awesome to have, but being online is different from being in face-to-face situations, and there are different rules. Play it safe and smart by following these tips when you're online:

1. Be cautious—people aren't always who they say they are online.

2. Don't share your name or address with anyone online.

3. Don't say or do anything online that you wouldn't say or do in person.

4. Always remember that what you say or do on social media cannot be undone.

5. Bullying is bullying, even if it is in writing online.

6. Remember, people can "share" what you say and do online.

7. If someone makes you uncomfortable online, trust your feelings and tell your parents!

8. Pay attention to how much time you are spending on social media.

9. If you always feel bad after being on social media, take a break for a few days, weeks, or more.

10. Only "follow" people who are uplifting and make you feel good.

YOU CRACKED THE CODE!

In this chapter, we talked about how to use social skills to know how to behave and act in class, when playing with others, and even when talking to adults.

In this chapter, you learned how to:

- Ask questions in class following the rules of social expectations
- Build your confidence around talking to adults
- Be a team player and a good sport when playing with others
- Be kind to people you know and to those you don't know
- Behave in class following the rules of social expectations

Next, in our final chapter, we'll talk about how to act at home and in other people's homes. You'll learn:

- How to share, even when it is a struggle
- When you should ask for permission to do something
- What things should be private and what things don't have to be
- How to make a good impression on others
- How to have good table manners
- How to be an awesome helper

Let's go put the final touches on your social skill superpowers!

Chapter Seven

AT HOME AND IN OTHER HOMES

We just learned that social skills help us know how to behave at school and in the classroom. Now let's explore how social skills can help us at home and in other people's homes.

Often, friendships mean play dates and sleepovers. How you behave at your house and in the homes of others is super important.

Have you ever invited someone over to your house only to be disappointed by how they behaved? Play dates and sleepovers can really put your social skill superpowers to the ultimate test. Can you share? Can you be flexible and cooperative? Can you have good manners and be considerate?

In this chapter, I am going to walk you through the Dos and Don'ts of surviving and thriving in your home and in others' homes.

SHARING EXPERIMENT

Sharing might be a little tricky at school, but at home it can be a completely different story! Your room is probably full of toys and treasures that you love, creations you built, and projects you are working on. For some kids, having another person in your space, touching all your things, can be really stressful.

Here's the tricky thing: One way to really destroy a play date or sleepover is to keep telling your friend not to touch your things. Sharing in this situation can be pretty hard, but it is really important for your friend to have a good time, or it could damage your friendship. But I've got an activity that can help.

Directions

It can definitely be helpful to plan the visit before your friends come over. That way, there are no surprises and you can focus on having fun! Answer the questions that follow so you can prepare for when friends come to your home.

I do not want my friends to touch these things (leave blank if you don't have anything to list):

- -

- -

- -

In order to make sure my friends don't touch these things, I can put them here (list the various places you can put these items so they're not out in the open):

- -

- -

- -

When my friends come over, we can play with these items:

- -

- -

- -

Awesome! Having a plan in place will help you feel less overwhelmed when your friends come over. Also, knowing which items or toys you want out of sight *before* your friends get there can help you avoid stressful moments.

BONUS ACTIVITY

It can help to practice sharing before you have someone over to your house. This can help you get used to the idea of other people touching your stuff.

Pick a small toy that you love. Ask a friend if they would like to borrow it for a day. You can tell them that you like to share and you thought they might enjoy playing with it.

How did your friend react? People usually love when others offer to share!

How did you feel? Were you relaxed? Nervous? If you had strong, uncomfortable feelings about this activity, you actually might want to do it more often! When we do things that make us uncomfortable more often, we eventually get used to the feeling. And when friends return things that they borrow, we become more comfortable with sharing.

This experiment will get you used to sharing so that when you have a play date, sharing will come more easily to you.

THE SHOULD OR SHOULDN'T GAME

Every house has different rules because every family is unique—and so are their rules.

When you are at someone else's home, though, there are some general rules that you should follow even if they aren't rules at your home.

Here are some examples of what you would need permission for at someone else's home:

* Taking food from the refrigerator, countertop, or pantry
* Eating food in a room other than the kitchen
* Turning on the TV
* Using their computer
* Going into other people's bedrooms
* Leaving the house to walk around the neighborhood
* Feeding their pets

If you did the things listed here without permission at your friend's house, they might think you are rude or don't have good manners. We don't want people to think that! This is why it's good to learn ahead of time what you can do with permission and without permission.

Directions

First, let's explore the rules in your home. Write down five things that require you to get permission:

1. _____

_____

2. _____

_____

3. _____

_____

4. _____

_____

5. _____

_____

THE SHOULD OR SHOULDN'T GAME, *continued*

Now, let's explore how well you understand what you need permission for at *other* people's homes. Circle "Yes" (you *do* need permission) or "No" (you *do not* need permission) next to each situation in the following list. See how you did by checking the answer key on page 121.

1. You see a good movie on the shelf. You want to watch it.   Yes   No

2. You have to go the bathroom.   Yes   No

3. You are hungry. You would love to get a snack.   Yes   No

4. Your friend's dog is begging for food. You want to feed it.   Yes   No

5. You want to visit another friend down the street.   Yes   No

6. You have your own phone and you want to call home.   Yes   No

7. You want to see what your friend's parents' bedroom looks like.   Yes   No

8. You want to call your mom and you see their phone.   Yes   No

9. You want to sit down and relax for a minute.   Yes   No

10. You want to go in the backyard and jump on their trampoline.   Yes   No

11. You feel dirty and want to take a shower before bed.   Yes   No

12. The dog is sitting at your feet and you want to pet it.   Yes   No

13. You are thirsty and want to pour yourself a drink.   Yes   No

14. You want to play a video game and you see the controller on the couch.   Yes   No

Answer Key

1. Y 2. N 3. Y 4. Y 5. Y 6. N 7. Y 8. Y 9. N 10. Y 11. Y 12. N 13. Y 14. Y

PRIVACY, PLEASE!

When we are in our own home, we do things that are pretty private. You probably feel relaxed in your own home, so you might do things there that you wouldn't normally do at school or in someone else's home. There are things, however, that you *should* do privately in your home if your friends are around because if you don't, they might feel awkward and uncomfortable.

It's good to know what to do privately when others are watching, especially friends!

Directions

Below is a list of behaviors. Some should definitely be done privately, and others can be done with other people watching. Mark the ones that you think should be private with an X.

1. Take off your clothes to change.

2. Pick your teeth, cut your toenails, or apply deodorant.

3. Call your mom.

4. Go to the bathroom.

5. Pick your nose.

6. Scratch your head.

7. Pick your underwear out of your bottom.

8. Scratch an itch on your arm.

9. Scratch your private parts.

10. Fart or burp.

Answer Key

1, 2, 4, 5, 7, 9, and 10 should all be done in private. Of course, if #10 happens accidentally, excusing yourself is an appropriate response.

How did you do? Were there any surprises? Don't be worried if there were, since learning is what this is all about! So next time you're with a friend, you'll know exactly what behaviors should be kept private.

I AIM TO IMPRESS!

Making a good impression on people is important. A "good impression" is how positive someone feels about you based on how you present yourself. If you are kind, considerate, and friendly, you are going to make a good impression. If you are rude or unfriendly, you are probably not going to make the best impression.

When you meet new kids, new teachers, and new adults, you are making a first impression. A first impression can affect whether or not someone wants to be your friend.

What kind of impression do you want to make? Check how you want others to view you when you first meet:

- ❏ Nice

- ❏ Thoughtful

- ❏ Polite

- ❏ Smart

- ❏ Neat

- ❏ Organized

- ❏ Curious

- ❏ Funny

- ❏ Kind

- ❏ Considerate of others

- ❏ Grateful

- ❏ Fill in: _____

I AIM TO IMPRESS!, *continued*

Directions

Pick three things from the previous list. Let's talk about how you can make that kind of impression on others. Fill in the blanks.

EXAMPLE

What are some ways you can show that you are ___*nice*___ [fill in a word you picked]?

I can be friendly and ask them how their day is going.

NOW IT'S YOUR TURN!

What are some ways you can show that you are _____ [fill in a word you picked]?

I can _____.

What are some ways you can show that you are _____ [fill in a word you picked]?

I can _____.

What are some ways you can show that you are _____ [fill in a word you picked]?

I can _____.

SERVING UP GOOD TABLE MANNERS

Part of having good social skills is having good table manners. How you act when you're eating can make a really big impression on others. Remember how we talked about making a good impression in our last activity? Well, one way or another, table manners definitely leave an impression—so you want it to be a good one!

Here are just a few things you can do that show good table manners:

Wash your hands and face before eating.	Put a napkin in your lap.
Don't start eating until everyone is seated and begins to eat.	Sit quietly (or join in if you wish) during any blessings or "grace."
Ask to be excused before leaving the table.	Chew with your mouth closed.
Don't talk with your mouth full.	Don't slurp your soup or drinks.
Don't reach over people for food. Ask politely for them to pass what you want.	Ask permission before taking more food.
Keep your napkin in your lap and use it to wipe your face and hands as you eat.	Use your fork, not your fingers, unless you've been served "finger food."
Say "please" and "thank you."	Bring your plate to the sink when you're done eating.
Bonus points: Thank the host for having you to dinner.	Bonus points: Compliment the cook.

SERVING UP GOOD TABLE MANNERS, *continued*

Directions

Mike invited his friend Jenny over for dinner. Mike isn't making a very good impression! Can you circle and label some of his bad table manners?

Answer Key

Mike isn't wiping his face, he is talking with his mouth full, he doesn't have his napkin on his lap, he is reaching over his friend for food, and he is not using his fork to eat his steak.

CAN I GIVE YOU A HAND?

When you have a friend over, there are many ways you can make them feel more comfortable. Friends might need help finding things around your house, and they might feel too nervous or awkward to ask. You can be a great friend by giving them a hand.

Here are some things friends might need help with when they are visiting your home:

- Having a snack
- Finding the bathroom
- Turning on the TV
- Using a phone to call home
- Logging in to your game console
- Finding your room

When you show your friend how to do these things, they are going to enjoy their visit and feel more relaxed at your home.

When you are over at your friend's home, you can be a different kind of helper. You can help your friend or their parents do many things. Offering to help shows really good manners and leaves a wonderful impression not only on your friend, but on your friend's parents as well!

Here are just a few ways you can offer to help:

- Say you'd like to help clean up
- Help clear the table after a meal
- Include your friend's siblings while playing

CAN I GIVE YOU A HAND?, *continued*

Directions

In each finger of the hand below, write something you could do to give a helping hand, either to your friend when they come to visit you, or when you are at a friend's house.

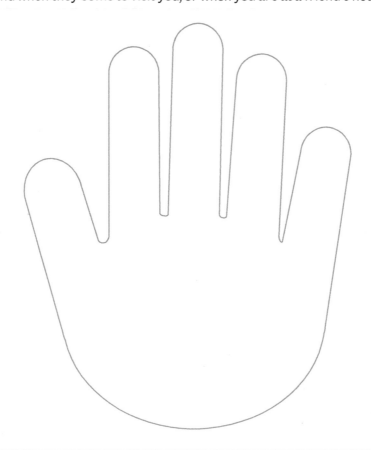

BONUS ACTIVITY

The next time you have a friend over, pick a few of the ideas you listed and try them out. Did your friend seem grateful? Did they seem more relaxed?

TOP 10 TIPS FOR BEING A GREAT GUEST

Visiting someone else's home can be fun. And if we have fun, we want to be invited back, right? Here are some things you can do to be the kind of guest that people want to invite back again and again.

1. Say "please" and "thank you."

2. Help clean up any messes.

3. Share toys with your friend.

4. Offer to include your friend's brothers and sisters.

5. Stay off your cell phone.

6. Answer questions with more than just a "yes" or "no."

7. Use good table manners when eating.

8. Offer to give people a hand if they need it.

9. Take turns and be flexible.

10. Don't shout, run around the house, or climb on furniture.

COLLAGE OF MY NEW TALENTS

We have come to our final activity! And through our journey, you've grown so many social superpowers. As a final goodbye, I want you to celebrate all that you have learned throughout this book. What are the biggest superpowers you grew?

Directions

What are the three biggest or best things you learned from doing all these activities?

1. --

----

2. --

----

3. --

Let's make a collage of the things you learned on the following page. Cut out pictures from a magazine or draw all the skills you learned. You can draw a picture of you sharing, showing good manners, or talking and meeting new friends. You can write or cut out words or symbols that remind you of what you learned.

Hang up the collage in your room as a reminder of how far you've come!

YOU CRACKED THE CODE!

Your social skill superpowers are now supercharged and ready to take on the world, or at least your school and neighborhood! You learned lots of tips about how to behave in other people's homes, and even in your own home.

In this chapter, you learned:

- How to share toys when you are hanging out with a friend
- When to ask for permission and when it isn't needed
- What things should be done privately
- How to make a good impression
- How to have great table manners
- How to give others a hand

In this book, we went from just learning what social skills are to learning how to talk to anybody. You learned how to be an awesome listener and how to use that superpower to make and keep friends. You took all those great skills and learned how to use them in school, out of school, and even in other people's homes.

You are well prepared to make and keep friends and make an excellent first, second, and third impression on both kids and grown-ups. But don't worry if you ever feel stumped or confused about how to handle a situation. Relationships, and especially friendships, can be challenging at times. Luckily you will always have this book as a great resource to read again and again. I'm so proud of you for your hard work, and I know that you are going to be awesome out there. And now that you have worked hard to develop social skill superpowers, you'll have them for life!

RESOURCES

WEBSITES

Social Emotional Developmental Checklists for Kids and Teens

KiddieMatters.com/social-emotional-development-checklists-for-kids-and-teens

5 Ways to Improve Your Child's Social Skills

Flintobox.com/blog/parenting/5-ways-to-improve-your-childs-social-skills-parenting

6 Ways to Improve Your Child's Social Skills

blog.BrainBalanceCenters.com/2017/06/6-ways-improve-childs-social-skills

Teaching Kids Social Skills When They Have None

AnxiousToddlers.com/social-skills

BOOKS

101 Ways to Teach Children Social Skills by Lawrence Shapiro

104 Activities That Build: Self-Esteem, Teamwork, Communication, Anger Management, Self-Discovery, Coping Skills by Alanna Jones

Making Friends Is an Art! by Julia Cook (children's book)

My Mouth Is a Volcano! by Julia Cook (children's book)

Personal Space Camp by Julia Cook (children's book)

Social Rules for Kids: The Top 100 Social Rules Kids Need to Succeed by Susan Diamond

Sorry, I Forgot to Ask! by Julia Cook (children's book)

INDEX

ABOUT THE AUTHOR

Natasha Daniels is a child therapist and mom to three kids who teach her most of what she knows in life. She is the author of *Anxiety Sucks! A Teen Survival Guide* and *How to Parent Your Anxious Toddler*. She is also the creator of the parenting site AnxiousToddlers.com.